CONTENTS

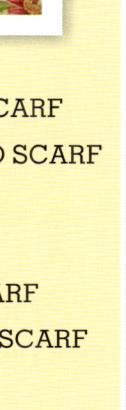

10

14

31

23

45

54

LOFTY LUSTER SCARF

MEASUREMENTS
Approximately 12 x 70"/30.5 x 177.5cm

GAUGE
10 sts and 14 rows to 4"/10cm over garter st in stripe pat, using size 10 (6mm) needles.
TAKE TIME TO CHECK GAUGE.

STITCH GLOSSARY
STRIPE PATTERN
*K 1 row in A, k 1 row in B, k 1 row in C; rep from * for stripe pat.

NOTE
To avoid tangling yarns, be sure to turn work clockwise at the end of each RS row and counterclockwise at the end of each WS row.

SCARF
With A, cast on 30 sts.

BEG STRIPE PAT
Work in garter st (k every row) and stripe pat until scarf measures approx 70"/177.5cm, end with a C row. Bind off.

TOOLKIT

YARN (4)
- 1¾oz/50g, 115yd/105m of any worsted weight mohair blend in magenta (A)
- 3oz/85g, 100yd/91m of any worsted weight mohair blend ribbon in dark pink (B)
- 1¾oz/50g, 88yd/80m of any worsted weight sparkle wool in red (C)

NEEDLES
- One pair size 10 (6mm) needles OR SIZE TO OBTAIN GAUGE

Paul Amato

SEED AND RIBBED SCARF

TOOLKIT

YARN 4
- 7oz/200g, 330yd/300m of any worsted weight wool

NEEDLES
- One pair size 8 (5mm) needles OR SIZE TO OBTAIN GAUGE.

MEASUREMENTS
72 x 7½"/182 x 19cm

GAUGE
14 sts x 23 rows to 4"/10cm over seed stitch.
TAKE TIME TO CHECK GAUGE.

STITCH GLOSSARY
SEED STITCH
(over an even number of sts)
Row 1 (RS) *K1, p1; rep from * to end.
Row 2 *P1, k1; rep from * to end
Rep rows 1 and 2 for seed stitch.

SCARF
Cast on 26 sts and work in seed stitch for 7½"/19cm. Work in k2, p2 rib as foll:
Row 1 Sl 1 st knitwise, k1, *p2, k2; rep from * to end.
Row 2 Sl 1 st purlwise, p1, *k2, p2; rep from * to end. Rep rows 1 and 2 for rib until piece measures 57"/145cm from beg. Work in seed stitch for 7½"/19cm. Bind off in pat.

Jenny Acheson

BAMBOO SCARF

TOOLKIT

YARN
- 7oz/200g, 240yd/220m of any bulky weight wool and acrylic blend

NEEDLES
- One pair size 10½ (6.5mm) needles OR SIZE TO OBTAIN GAUGE

MEASUREMENTS
60 x 5¼"/152.5cm x 13.5cm

GAUGE
18 sts and 16 rows (unstretched) to 4"/10cm over bamboo stitch.
TAKE TIME TO CHECK GAUGE.

STITCH GLOSSARY
BAMBOO STITCH
(multiple of 6 sts)
Rows 1, 3, 7, and 9 (RS) *P2, k4; rep from * to end.
Rows 2, 4, 8, and 10 (WS) *P4, k2; rep from * to end.
Row 5 *P8, k4; rep from * to end.
Row 6 *P4, k8; rep from * to end.
Row 11 P2, *k4, p8; rep from *, end p6.
Row 12 K6, * p4, k8; rep from *, end k2.
Rep rows 1–12 for bamboo stitch.

SCARF
Cast on 24 sts. Work in bamboo stitch until piece measures 60"/152.5cm. Bind off.

Paul Amato

TOOLKIT

YARN

- (5) 10½oz/300g, 180yd/165m of any bulky weight wool in green (MC)
- 3½oz/100g, 60yd/54m in pale lilac (A)
- (3) 1¾oz/50g, 219yd/200m of any DK weight wool in lilac (B)
- .88oz/25g, 229yd/210m of any DK weight mohair blend in purple (C)

NEEDLES

- One pair size 13 (9mm) needles OR SIZE TO OBTAIN GAUGE

Quenet

KNITTED MEASUREMENTS
Approx 8 x 72"/20.5 x 183cm

GAUGE
16 sts and 14 rows to 4"/10cm over pat st using MC and size 13 (9mm) needles.
TAKE TIME TO CHECK GAUGE

STITCH GLOSSARY
PATTERN STITCH
(multiple of 6 sts plus 3)
Row 1 (RS) K3, *p3, k3; rep from * to end.
Row 2 P1, *k1, p1; rep from * to end.
Rep rows 1 and 2 for pat st.

SCARF
With MC, cast on 27 sts. Work in pat st for 72"/183cm from beg. Bind off.

FLOWERS
(make 2 each in A, B, and C)
Note When working flowers, use 2 strands B held tog and 3 strands C held tog.
Cast on 56 sts.
Row 1 (RS) Knit.
Row 2 P2tog across—28 sts.
Row 3 Knit.
Row 4 Purl.
Row 5 K2tog across—14 sts.
Row 6 Purl.
Row 7 K2tog across—7 sts.
Cut yarn, leaving 15"/38cm tail. Draw tail through rem sts and fasten off. Sew edges together. Allow outer edge to curl inward.

FLOWER CENTER (BOBBLE)
(make 6 in MC)
Cast on 1 st, leaving 15"/38cm tail.

Row 1 (RS) K into front, back, front, back, front of st—5 sts.
Row 2 Purl.
Row 3 K1, SK2P, k1—3 sts.
Row 4 P3tog—1 st.
Cut yarn, leaving 15"/38cm tail. Fasten st.

FINISHING
Place bobble in center of flower. Pull the 2 ends through flower and tie a knot on WS. Place flower on scarf in desired position. Pull 2 ends of bobble through scarf and tie a knot on WS. Rep for other flowers, attaching 3 flowers to each end of scarf.

TOOLKIT

YARN

- ⑤ 10½oz/300g, 330yd/300m of any bulky weight wool in red (MC)
- ⑥ 5¾oz/150g, 110yd/100m of any super-bulky weight wool in cream (CC)

NEEDLES

- One pair each sizes 8 and 11 (5mm and 8mm) needles OR SIZE TO OBTAIN GAUGE

OTHER

- Tapestry needle, fabric glue and crochet hook

MEASUREMENTS

Approximately 7 x 60"/18 x 152.5cm (not including fringe)

GAUGE

15 sts and 30 rows to 4"/10cm over garter st using smaller needles and MC.
TAKE TIME TO CHECK GAUGE.

SCARF

With MC and smaller needles, cast on 25 sts. Work in garter st (knit every row) for 3"/7.5cm. *Join CC and k 2 rows. [K 2 rows MC, k 2 rows CC] twice, cut CC*. Cont in garter st with MC only for 4"/10cm more. Rep between *'s once Cont in garter st With MC only for 40"/101.5cm. Rep between *'s once. Cont in garter st with MC only for 4"/10cm more. Rep between *'s once. Cont in garter st with MC only for 3"/7.5cm. Bind off.

FINISHING

FRINGE

Cut 54 lengths of CC each 15"/38cm long. With 3 strands held tog, fold in half and using crochet hook, pull loop through a st on cast-on or bound-off edge. Pull ends of strands through loop. Make 9 for each end. Trim even.

NORWEGIAN STARS

With larger needles and CC, cast on 30 sts. In St st (knit on RS, purl on WS) use entire skein of CC to make a rectangle.

FELTING

Put completed rectangle in washing machine set to hot wash/cold rinse with low water level. Add one tablespoon dishwashing detergent and ¼ cup baking soda at beginning of wash cycle. Repeat the cycle, if necessary, until piece is felted smooth. Squeeze out excess water and pin flat to dry. Using Norwegian star template, cut pieces from felted square (make two of each). Set pieces into place on scarf between each striped section and glue with fabric glue. Let dry. Pieces can also be sewn to scarf with needle and thread.

NORWEGIAN STAR TEMPLATE

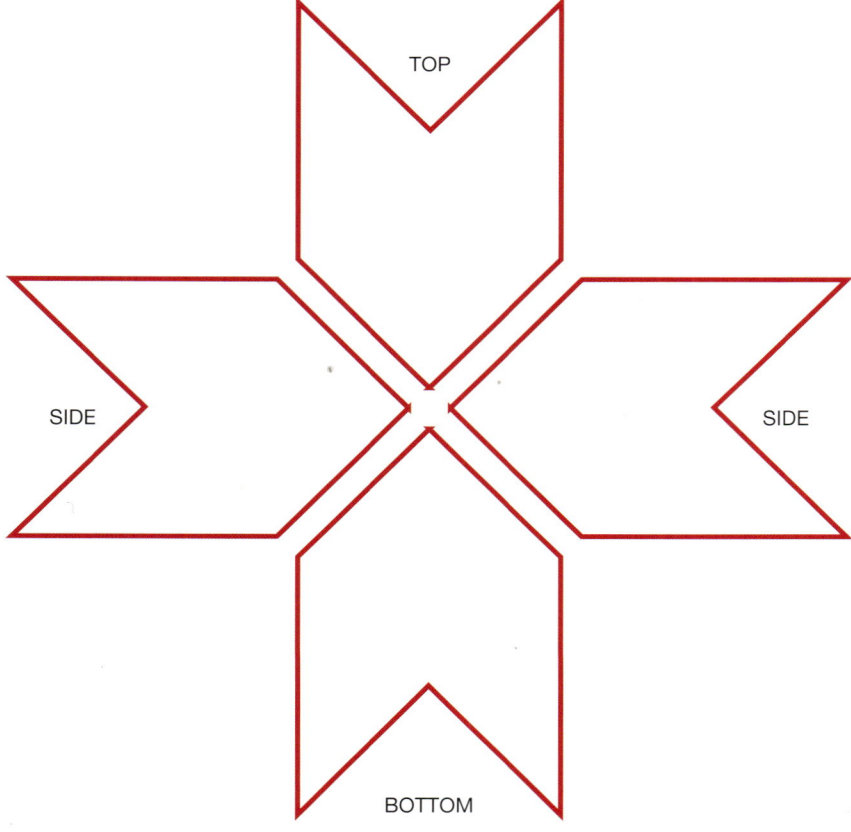

FLOWER POWER SCARF

TOOLKIT

YARN

- 10½oz/300g, 330yd/300m of any bulky weight wool in taupe (MC)
- Small amounts of bulky weight wool in teal (A) and black (B)

NEEDLES

- One pair size 11 (8mm) needles, OR SIZE TO OBTAIN GAUGE
- One extra size 11 (8mm) needle for 3-needle bind-off
- Two size 11 (7mm) double-pointed needles (dpns)

OTHER

- Felting needle and felting surface

MEASUREMENTS

9 x 76"/23 x 193cm (before felting, excluding fringe)
8 x 72"/20.5 x 183cm (after felting, excluding fringe)

GAUGE

11 sts and 16 rows to 4"/10cm over St st using size 11 (8mm) needles (before felting).
TAKE TIME TO CHECK GAUGE.

SPECIAL TECHNIQUE

3-NEEDLE BIND-OFF

1 Hold right sides of pieces together on two needles. Insert third needle knitwise into first st of each needle, and wrap yarn knitwise.
2 Knit these two sts together, and slip them off the needles. *Knit the next two sts together in the same manner.
3 Slip first st on 3rd needle over 2nd st and off needle. Rep from * in step 2 across row until all sts are bound off.

Note Scarf is knitted by making 7 individual I-cords and joining them in the first row. The two halves of the scarf are worked separately and joined in the middle with 3-needle bind off. The piece is then lightly felted by machine (approx 10% shrinkage) and embellished with needle felted flowers.

I-CORD FRINGE (make 7 for each end of scarf)

Using dpn and MC, cast on 3 sts.
***Next row (RS)** With 2nd dpn, k3, do not turn. Slide sts to beg of needle. Pull yarn firmly across back and repeat from * until cord measures 6"/15cm. Cut yarn and slip sts to a spare needle or stitch holder. Do not cut yarn on final cord for each half.

SCARF

FIRST HALF

*Knit across 3 I-cord stitches, cast on 1 st; rep from * until 7 cords are attached—27 sts.
Row 1 (WS) K3, p21, k3.
Row 2 (RS) K across. Rep rows 1 and 2 until scarf measures 38"/96.5cm (or half of desired total length, excluding fringe) ending with a WS row. Cut yarn and place all stitches on holder.

SECOND HALF

Work as for first half.

FINISHING

Join halves using 3-needle bind off with right sides together. Weave in all ends. With scarf in zippered pillowcase or lingerie bag, place in washing machine with a pair of old jeans to increase friction during agitation. Set machine to hot wash/cold rinse with low water level. Add 1 tablespoon dishwashing detergent and ¼ cup baking soda at beginning of wash cycle. Watch scarf closely during agitation, checking progress every few minutes. Remove scarf from washer when stitches appear fuzzy but still recognizable. Be careful not to overfelt. Rinse in cold water. Roll scarf in towels and squeeze to remove excess water. Pin out straight, stretching to measurements and adjusting fringe evenly. Leave pinned until thoroughly dry.

EMBELLISHING

Using diagram and working on felting surface, with B make small swirls for flower centers. Tack lightly in place with felting needle. With A, make flower petal designs around centers. Tack in place. At this point, designs can be removed and repositioned as desired. Place flowers and partial flowers randomly on scarf as desired. Once design placement is satisfactory, use felting tool to attach flower designs firmly.

NEEDLE FELTING DIAGRAM
(Actual Size)

LACE SCARF

MEASUREMENTS

15 x 67"/38 x 70cm (without fringe)

GAUGE

18 sts and 26 rows to 4"/10cm over lace pat using size 7 (4.5mm) needles after blocking. **TAKE TIME TO CHECK GAUGE.**

STITCH GLOSSARY

LACE PATTERN
(multiple of 4 sts)
Row 1 Sl 1, k3, *k2, yo, k2tog; rep from *to last 4 sts, end k3, k1 tbl.
Rep row 1 for lace pat.

SCARF

Note Slip the first stitch of each row with yarn in front then bring yarn to back between first and 2nd sts and knit.
Cast on 76 sts loosely.
Row 1 (WS) Sl 1 st, k to last st, k1 tbl. **Rows 2–7** Rep row 1.
Note Mark next row for RS. Work in lace pat until piece measures 66¼"/168cm from beg
Next 7 rows Work rows 1–7 same as beg of scarf. Bind off loosely

FINISHING

Block scarf.

FRINGE

Cut 20½"/52cm lengths of yarn. Thread 4 strands through yarn needle; insert needle into edge stitch and pull yarn halfway through. Remove needle, line up ends of strands, then tie fringe into single knot close to edge of wrap. Tie one 4-strand fringe at each corner, and at each end of solid columns of sts. Tie 2 more knots in fringe at 2"/5cm apart. Trim ends of fringe to measure 2"/5cm below final knot.

TOOLKIT

YARN

- 7oz/200g, 680yd/620m of any sport weight wool and cotton blend

NEEDLES

- One pair size 7 (4.5mm) needles OR SIZE TO OBTAIN GAUGE

OTHER

- Stitch marker

Paul Amato

BASIC BLUE SCARF

MEASUREMENTS
Approximately 6 x 64½"/15 x 164cm

GAUGES
22 sts and 25 rows to 4"/10cm over pattern st using size 9 (5.5mm) needles.
7 rows to 3½"/9cm over crochet edging using size I/9 (5.5mm) hook.
TAKE TIME TO CHECK GAUGES.

TOOLKIT

YARN
- 7oz/200g, 380yd/340m of any worsted weight wool

NEEDLES
- One pair size 9 (5.5mm) needles OR SIZE TO OBTAIN GAUGE

OTHER
- Size I/9 (5.5mm) crochet hook

STITCH GLOSSARY
PATTERN STITCH
(multiple of 6 sts plus 2, plus 2 edge sts)
Row 1 (RS) K1 tbl, p2, *k4, p2; rep from *, end k1.
Rows 2 and 4 Sl 1 purlwise, *k2, p4; rep from * to the last st, sl 1 purlwise.
Row 3 Rep row 1.
Rows 5 and 7 K1 tbl, k3, p2, *k4, p2; rep from * to last 4 sts, k4.
Rows 6 and 8 Sl 1 purlwise, p3, k2, *p4, k2; rep from * to last 4 sts, p3, sl 1 purlwise.
Rep rows 1–8 for pattern stitch.

SCARF
Cast on 34 sts. Work in pat st until work measures 57½"/146cm from beg, end with a row 3 or 7. Bind off in pat on row 4 or 8. Do not cut yarn, insert crochet hook into last loop.

BORDER
Row 1 Ch 1, sc in first st (same sp as ch 1), *ch 2, skip next 2 sts, sc in next st; rep from * to end, ending last rep with sc in sl st—11 ch-2 sps. Turn.
Row 2 Ch 3, 2 dc in ch-2 sp, *ch 1, 3 dc in ch-2 sp; rep from *, end last rep with 2 dc in last ch-2 sp, dc in last sc. Turn.
Rows 3, 5 and 7 Ch 1, sc in fist sc, ch 3, skip 2 dc, sc in next ch-1 sp (between dc groups), *ch 3, skip 3 dc, sc into ch-1 sp (between dc groups); rep from *, omitting sc in ch-1 sp in last rep, sc in 3rd ch of t-ch. Turn.
Rows 4 and 6 Ch 3, 2 dc in first ch-3 sp *ch 1, 3 dc in next ch-3 sp; rep from * ending last rep with 2 sc in last ch-3 sp, dc in last sc. Turn.
Row 7 Ch 5, *sc in ch-1 sp (between dc groups), ch 4; rep from *, ending with sl st in 3rd ch of t-ch. Fasten off.
Rep border for opposite end, rejoining yarn at RH edge.

BIASED SCARF

Paul Amato

TOOLKIT

YARN 4

- 8oz/230g, 450yd/415m of any worsted weight wool

NEEDLES

- One pair size 7 (4.5mm) needles OR SIZE TO OBTAIN GAUGE

MEASUREMENTS

Approximately 6 x 90"/15 x 229cm

GAUGE

17 sts and 21 rows to 4"/10cm over lace pattern using size 7 (4.5mm) needles. TAKE TIME TO CHECK GAUGE.

STITCH GLOSSARY

LACE PATTERN (multiple of 3 sts plus 2)
Row 1 (RS) K2, *k1, ssk, yo; rep from *, end k3.
Rows 2 and 4 K1, p to last st, k1.
Row 3 K2, *ssk, yo, k1; rep from* to end.
Row 5 K1,*ssk, yo, k1; rep from*, end k1.
Row 6 Rep row 2.
Rep rows 1–6 for lace pat.

SCARF

Cast on 2 sts.

BEG CHART 1
Row 1 (RS) Knit.
Row 2 (WS) Purl.
Row 3 K1, yo, k1.
Row 4 and all WS rows K1, p to last st, k1.
Row 5 K1, yo, k2. Cont to work chart in this way, therefore inc 1 st at beg of every RS row, through row 52—27 sts.
Row 53 (RS) K1, [k1, ssk, yo] 8 times, ssk—26 sts.
Row 54 Rep row 4. Cont to rep rows 55–60 for working even in lace pat, until piece measures approx 81"/206cm from beg, end with a pat row 56.

BEG CHART 2
Row 1 (RS) K3, [ssk, yo, k1] 7 times, ssk—25 sts. Cont in chart pat in this way through row 47. Bind off rem 2 sts.

CHART 1

6-row rep

STITCH KEY

- ☐ k on RS, p on WS
- ⊟ p on RS, k on WS
- ⋉ ssk
- ⊡ yo

CHART 2

26 sts

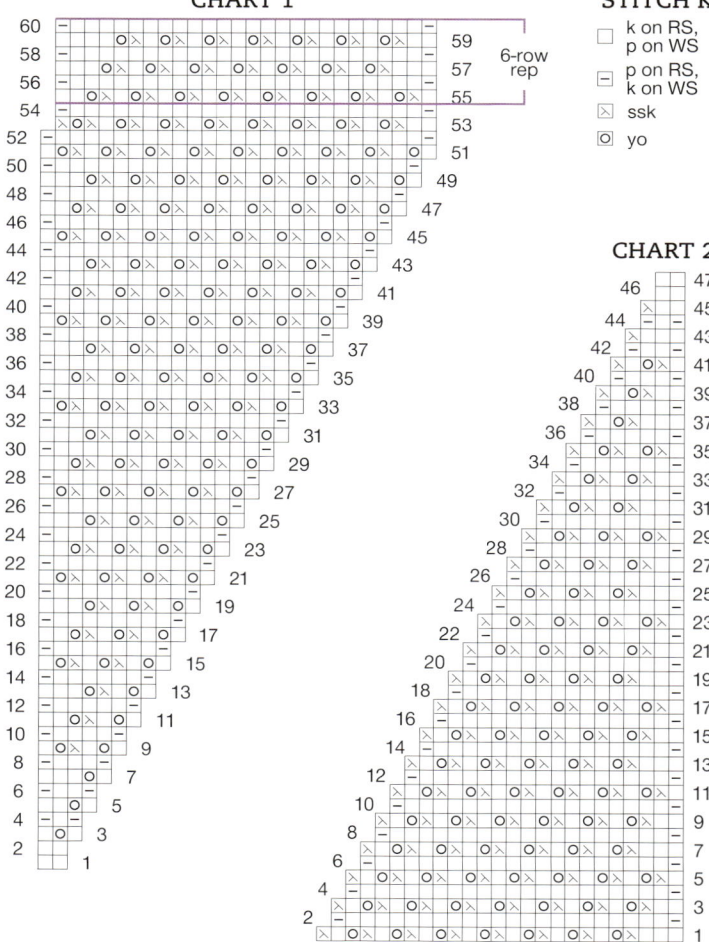

TRIANGLE EYELET SHAWL

TOOLKIT

YARN

- 8¾oz/250g, 770yd/700m of any worsted weight wool blend

NEEDLES

- One pair size 6 (4mm) needles OR SIZE TO OBTAIN GAUGE GAUGE

MEASUREMENTS
Width at upper edge 50½"/128cm
Length at center back 27½"/70cm

GAUGE
22 sts and 40 rows to 4"/10cm over garter and lace pat using size 6 (4mm) needles.
TAKE TIME TO CHECK GAUGE.

SHAWL
Place slip knot on needle.
Row 1 (RS) K in front, back and front of st—3 sts.
Row 2 Knit.
Note To make edge neat and even, pull tightly on yarn after slipping st at beg of every row.
Row 3 Sl 1 knitwise, k in front, back and front of st—5 sts.
Row 4 Sl 1 purlwise, knit to end.
Row 5 Sl 1 purlwise, k1, yo, k to last 2 sts, yo, k2—7 sts.
Row 6 Rep row 4.
Rows 7–14 Rep rows 5 and 6 four times—15 sts.
Row 15 Rep row 5—17 sts.
Lace row 16 (WS) Sl 1 purlwise, p1, *yo, p2tog; rep from *, end k1.
Rows 17 and 19 Rep row 5—21 sts.
Row 18 Sl 1 purlwise, knit to end.

Row 20 Rep lace row 16.
Rows 21–35 Rep rows 5 and 6 seven times, then row 5 once more—37 sts.
Rep rows 16–35 (20 rows) 12 times more—277 sts.
K 1 row on WS, Bind off loosely.

Paul Amato

FRENCH SCARF

■■■□

MEASUREMENTS
Width (widest point) 11½"/29cm
Width (narrowest point) 4½"/11.5cm
Length 69"/175cm

GAUGE
16 sts and 21 rows to 4"/10cm over St st using size 8 (5mm) needles.
TAKE TIME TO CHECK GAUGE

TOOLKIT

YARN ④
- 3½oz/100g, 210yd/190m of any worsted weight variegated wool and acrylic blend in dark grey (A) and light grey (B)

NEEDLES
- One pair size 8 (5mm) needles OR SIZE TO OBTAIN GAUGE
- Two size 8 (5mm) double pointed needles (dpns)

STITCH GLOSSARY
Pfb
Increase by purling into the front and then the back loop of the same stitch.
Note All color changes are worked on RS.

SCARF
With A, cast on 48 sts.
Rows 1–22 [K8, p8] 3 times.
Dec row 23 (RS) [K2, ssk] twice, p8, k8, p8, [k2tog, k2] twice, p8.
Dec row 24 [K2, ssk] twice, p6, k8, p8, [k2tog, k2] twice, p6—40 sts.
Dec row 25 [K1, ssk] twice, p6, k8, p8, [k2tog, k1] twice, p6—36 sts.
Dec row 26 [K1, ssk] twice, p4, k8, p8, [k2tog, k1] twice, p4—32 sts.
Change to B and work next 18 rows as foll: k4, p4, k8, p8 k4, p4.
Next (dec) row (RS) K2, ssk, p4, k8, p8, k2tog, k2, p4—30 sts.
Next (dec) row K2, ssk, p3, k8, p8, k2tog, k2, p3—28 sts.
Change to A and work 14 rows as foll: k3, p3, k8, p8, k3, p3.
Next (dec) row (RS) K1, ssk, p3, k8, p8, k2tog, k1, p3—26 sts.
Next (dec) row K1, ssk, p2, k8, p8, k2tog, k1, p2—24 sts. Change to B and work 8 rows as foll: K2, p2, k8, p8, k2, p2.
Next (dec) row (RS) Ssk, p2, k8, p8, k2tog, p2—22 sts.
Next row Ssk, p1, k8, p8, k2tog, p1—20 sts.
Change to A and work 6 rows as foll: K1, p1, k8, p8, k1, p1.
Next (dec) row (RS) K1, p1, k8, p8, k2tog—19 sts.
Next (dec) row p1, k8, p8, k2tog—18 sts. Change to B and work 6 rows as foll: P1, k8, p8, k1.
Next (dec) row (RS) K2tog, k7, p8, k1—17 sts.
Next row k2tog, k7, p8—16 sts.
Cont in established rib pat and, alternating A and

B, work 6 rows in each color for 24 rows, work 4 rows in each color for 24 rows, work 2 rows in each color for 40 rows, work 4 rows in each color for 24 rows, work 6 rows in each color for 24 rows. Change to A.
Next (inc) row (RS) K8, p7, pfb—17 sts.
Next (inc) row P1, k8, p7, pfb—18 sts Work next 6 rows as foll: P1, k8, p8, k1.
Change to B.
Next (inc) row (RS) Kfb, k8, p8, k1—19 sts.
Next (inc) row Kfb, k8, p8, k1, p1—20 sts. Work 6 rows as foll: K1, p1, K8, p8, k1, p1. Change to A.
Next (inc) row (RS) K1, M1, p1, k8, p8, k1, M1, p1—22 sts.
Next (inc) row K1, M1, p2, k8, p8, k1, M1, p2—24 sts. Work next 8 rows as foll: k2, p2, k8, p8, k2, p2. Change to B.
Next (inc) row (RS) K2, M1, p2, k8, p8, k2, M1 p-st, p2—26 sts.
Next (inc) row K3, M1 p-st, p2, k8, p8, k2, M1, p3—28 sts. Work next 14 rows as foll: k3, p3, k8, p8, k3, p3. Change to A.
Next (inc) row (RS) K3, M1, p3, k8, p8, k3, M1, p3—30 sts.
Next (inc) row K3, M1, p4, k8, p8, k4, M1 p-st, p3—32 sts. Work next 18 rows as foll: K4, p4, k8, p8, k4, p4. Change to B.
Next (inc) row (RS) K4, M1 p-st, k8, p8, k4, M1, p4—36 sts.
Next (inc) row K4, M1 p-st, p6, M1 p-st, K8, P8, M1, k6, M1, p4—40 sts.
Next (inc) row [K2, M1] twice, [p8, k2] twice, [M1 p-st, p2] twice—44 sts.
Next (inc) row [K2, M1] twice, k2, [p2, k8] twice, M1 p-st, p2, M1 p-st, p4—48 sts. Work next 22 rows as foll: [K8, p8] 3 times. Bind off.

FINISHING
I-CORD EDGING
With dpn and A, cast on 3 sts.
*Row 1 (RS) K3. Do not turn work. Slide sts to opposite end of needle to work next row from RS. Rep from * until cord measures 11"/28cm long. Bind off. Sew along cast-on edge of scarf. Work another cord with B and sew to bound-off edge of scarf.

AMERICAN SCARF

TOOLKIT

YARN 4
- 1¾oz/50g, 77yd/70m of any worsted weight wool in teal (A), lime green (B), light green (C), turquoise (D), light blue (E), and bright green (F)

NEEDLES
- One pair size 8 (5mm) needles OR SIZE TO OBTAIN GAUGE

Rose Callahan

MEASUREMENTS
4 x 48"/10 x 122cm (without pom poms)

GAUGE
18 sts and 34 rows to 4"/10cm over garter st using size 8 (5mm) needles.
TAKE TIME TO CHECK GAUGE.

SCARF
Note Always end each 4"/10cm stripe with a WS row so that color change is visible on WS only.
With A, cast on 18 sts. *Cont with A, work in garter st (knit every row) for 4"/10cm, end with a WS row. Work 4"/10cm stripes with B, C, D, E and F; rep from * once more. Bind off.

FINISHING
Make 2 pom poms each in colors A, B, D and F as foll: wind yarn around two fingers about 15 times. Cut yarn and remove from fingers. Tie a 12"/30.5cm piece of yarn tightly around middle of pom pom. Cut loops and trim ends so that pom pom measures ½"/1.5cm. Sew one of each color to each end of scarf.

LONG SCARF

TOOLKIT

YARN
- 7oz/200g, 330yd/300m of any worsted weight cotton

NEEDLES
- One pair size 7 (4.5mm) needles OR SIZE TO OBTAIN GAUGE

OTHER
- Safety pin

MEASUREMENTS
Approx 7 x 56"/17.5 x 142cm

GAUGE
18 sts and 24 rows to 4"/10cm over St st using size 7 (4.5 mm) needles. TAKE TIME TO CHECK GAUGE.

STITCH GLOSSARY
STRIPE PATTERN
*10 rows St st, 10 rows rev St st; rep from * (20 rows) for stripe pat.

SCARF
Cast on 3 sts and work in stripe pat as foll:
Row 1 (RS) Kfb, k to last st, kfb.
Row 2 Purl.
Rows 3–10 Rep rows 1 and 2 four times—13 sts.
Row 11 (K1, p1) in first st, p to last st, (p1, k1 tbl) in last st.
Row 12 Knit.
Rows 13–20 Rep rows 11 and 12 four times—23 sts.
Note Place safety pin on RS of work. Keep a careful count of the rows to determine when to change from St st to rev St st in the stripe pat.
Rows 21–40 Rep rows 1–20 once—43 sts. Piece measures approx 7"/17.5cm wide (measured along side edge). Cont to work even in stripe pat as foll: **Next row (RS)** Inc in first st, work to last 2 sts, k2tog. Work 1 row even. Rep last 2 rows until the long side measures approx 56"/142cm, end with a WS row.
Dec row (RS) Bind off 2 sts, work to last 2 sts, k2tog. Work 1 row even. Rep last 2 rows until all sts have been decreased. Fasten off.

FINISHING
Block piece lightly.

Rose Callahan

TOOLKIT

YARN (4)

- 7oz/200g, 370yd/340m of any worsted weight wool tweed

NEEDLES

- One pair size 9 (5.5mm) needles OR SIZE TO OBTAIN GAUGE

OTHER

- Cable needle (cn)

MEASUREMENTS

8 x 56"/20.5 x 142cm

GAUGE

18 sts and 24 rows to 4"/10cm over St st using size 9 (5.5mm) needles.
TAKE TIME TO CHECK YOUR GAUGE.

STITCH GLOSSARY

3-st LPC
Sl 2 sts to cn and hold to *front*, p1, k2 from cn.
3-st RPC
Sl 1 st to cn and hold to *back*, k2, p1 from cn.
4-st LC
Sl 2 sts to cn and hold to *front*, k2, k2 from cn.
4-st RC
Sl 2 sts to cn and hold to *back*, k2, k2 from cn.

BROKEN RIB

(multiple of 2 sts plus 1)
Row 1 (RS) Sl 1, *p1, k1; rep from * to end.
Row 2 Sl 1, p to end.
Rep rows 1 and 2 for broken rib.

SCARF

Cast on 41 sts. Work in broken rib for 2"/5cm, ending with a RS row.
Work set-up row of cable chart and inc where indicated—42 sts. Cont to work cable chart until rows 1–24 have been worked 13 times. Work rows 1–5 once more.
Next row (WS) Sl 1, p19, p2tog, p20—41 sts.
Work in broken rib for 2"/5cm, ending with a RS row. Bind off purlwise on WS.

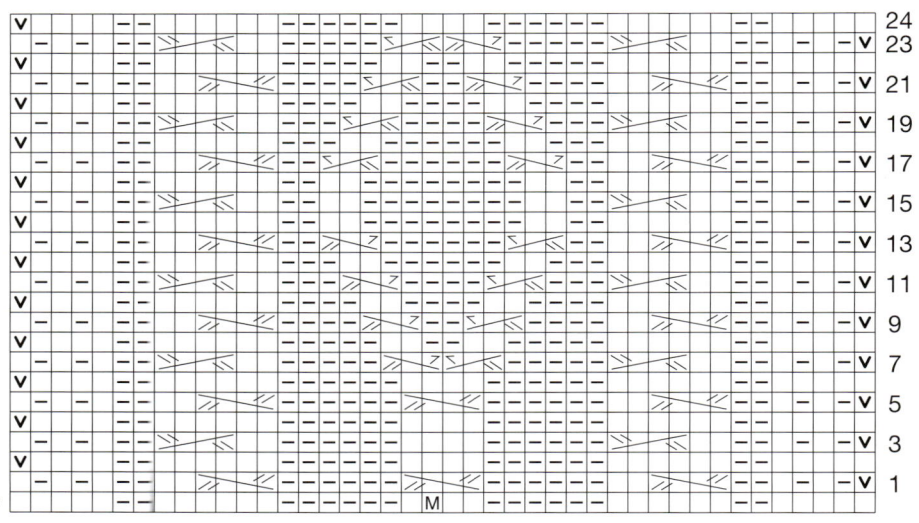

Set up row

STITCH KEY

☐ k on RS, p on WS	✓ slip st
⊟ p on RS, k on WS	M make 1

3-st RPC · 4-st RC
3-st LPC · 4-st LC

TOOLKIT

YARN

- 5¼oz/150g, 300yd/ 270m of any worsted weight cotton/acrylic blend

NEEDLES

- One pair size 4 (3.5mm) needles OR SIZE TO OBTAIN GAUGE

OTHER

- Stitch markers

MEASUREMENTS

Length 43½"/110.5cm
Width at center 5½"/14cm
Width at ends 10"/25.5cm

GAUGE

20 sts and 27 rows to 4"/10cm over St st using size 4 (3.5mm) needles.
TAKE TIME TO CHECK YOUR GAUGE.

STITCH GLOSSARY

Kfb
Inc 1 st by knitting into the front and back of same st.
Pbkf
Inc 1 st by purling in back loop, then knitting in front loop of same st.
M1
Insert LH needle under strand between st just worked and next st. Knit this strand, do NOT twist.
SK2P
Sl 1, k2tog, pass sl st over k2tog.

NOTES

1 Scarf is reversible.
2 Incs and decs are worked on both RS and WS throughout.
3 RS and WS reverse at beg of chart 2.

SCARF

Cast on 55 sts. Knit 2 rows.
Row 1 (WS) K5, [p5, k5] 5 times.
Row 2 (RS) K10, p5, [k5, p5] 3 times, k10.
Place marker on last row worked for RS of scarf.
Rep last 2 rows once, then row 1 once.
BEG CHART 1
Work rows 1–46 of chart 1—29 sts.
Next row (RS) K10, p9, k10.
Next row K5, p5, k9, p5, k5.
Rep last 2 rows until piece measures 35"/89cm from beg, end with a RS row.
Change marker to mark next row as a RS row.
BEG CHART 2
Work rows 1–47 of chart 2—55 sts.
Next row (WS) K10, [p5, k5] 3 times, p5, k10.
Next row [K5, p5] 5 times, k5.
Rep last 2 rows once more.
Knit 2 rows. Bind off.

Paul Amato

CHART 1
end with 29 sts

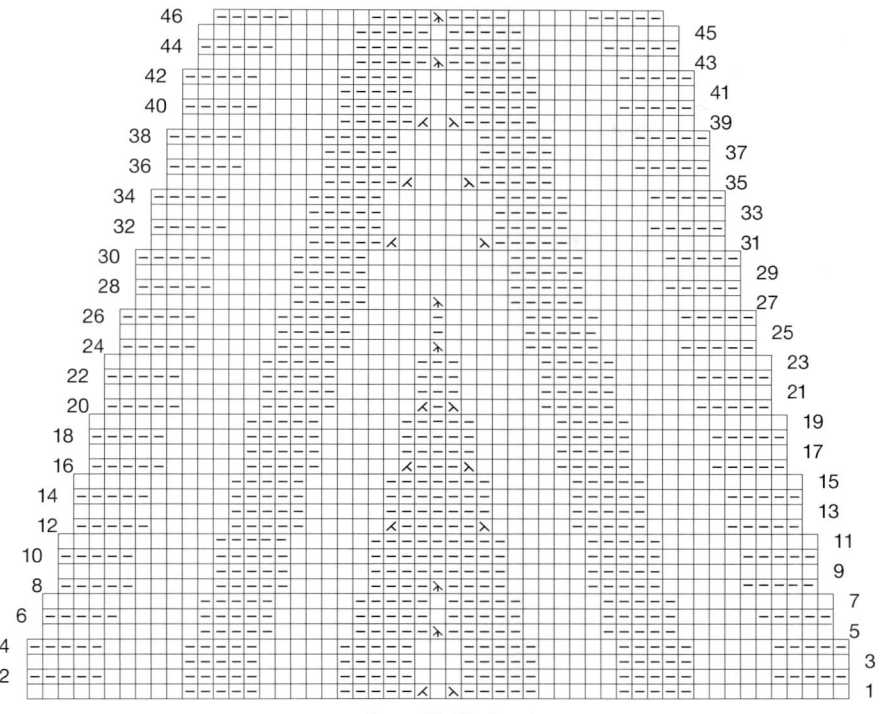

beg with 55 sts

CHART 2
end with 55 sts

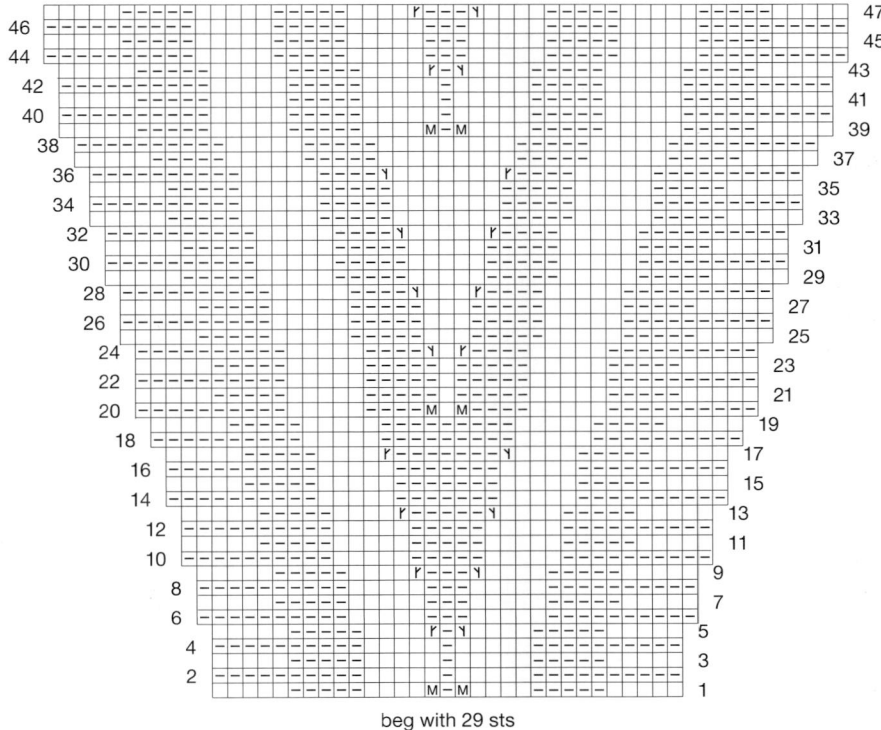

beg with 29 sts

STARRY NIGHT

TOOLKIT

YARN

- 3½oz/100g, 200yd/185m of any sport weight wool and acrylic blend with sequins

NEEDLES

- One pair size 9 (5.5mm) needles OR SIZE TO OBTAIN GAUGE

MEASUREMENTS

Approximately 6 x 62"/15 x 157.5cm

GAUGE

16 sts and 23 rows to 4"/10cm over St st after blocking using size 9 (5.5mm) needles. TAKE TIME TO CHECK GAUGE.

SCARF

Cast on 24 sts. Work 5 rows in garter st (k every row).

BEGIN CHART

Note that first chart rep begins on row 3. When first rep is complete, all 16 rows are worked.

Row 1 (RS) K3, work 6-st rep of chart row 3 times across, k3.

Row 2 K3, p to last 3 sts, k3.

Cont to work chart in this manner through row 16. Rep rows 1–16 until piece measures approx 61"/155cm from beg, end with a row 9. Work 5 rows in garter st. Bind off.

FINISHING

Block to measurements.

STITCH KEY

- ☐ k on RS, p on WS
- ⊠ k2tog
- ⊠ SKP
- ⊙ yo

6-st rep

Rose Callahan

TOOLKIT

YARN
- 7oz/200g, 485yd/450m of any DK weight wool

NEEDLES
- One pair size 9 (5.5mm) needles OR SIZE TO OBTAIN GAUGE

MEASUREMENTS
Approximately 13½ x 62"/34.5 x 157.5cm

GAUGE
15 sts and 20 rows to 4"/10cm over lace pat using size 9 (5.5mm) needles. TAKE TIME TO CHECK GAUGE.

STITCH GLOSSARY
LACE PATTERN (multiple of 2 plus 7)
Row 1 (RS) K4, *yo, k2tog; rep from * to the last 3 sts, k3.
Row 2 K4, purl to last 4 sts, k4.
Row 3 K3, *k2tog, yo; rep from * to the last 4 sts, k4.
Row 4 Rep row 2.
Row 5 K4, *yo, k2tog; rep from * to the last 3 sts, k3.
Rows 6-10 Knit.
Rep rows 1–10 for lace pattern.

WRAP
Cast on 51 sts. Knit 8 rows.
BEG LACE PAT
Work rows 1–10 of lace pat 29 times. Then rep rows 1–5 once more. Piece measures approx 61"/155cm from beg. Knit 8 rows. Bind off.

Paul Amato

DIAGONAL KEYHOLE

Rose Callahan

TOOLKIT

YARN

- 3½oz/100g, 230yd/210m of any DK weight variegated bamboo yarn

NEEDLES

- One pair size 6 (4mm) needles OR SIZE TO OBTAIN GAUGE GAUGE

MEASUREMENTS

Approximately 6 x 50"/15 x 127cm.

GAUGE

24 sts and 24 rows to 4"/10cm over pattern using size 6 (4mm) needles.
TAKE TIME TO CHECK GAUGE.

SCARF

Cast on 36 sts.
Row 1 (RS) K2, [ssk, k6, yo, p3] 3 times, k1.
Row 2 K1, [k3, p8] 3 times, k2.

Rep last 2 rows until scarf measures 18"/45.5cm from beg.

BEG KEYHOLE OPENING

Next (RS) row Work 13 sts in pat and place sts on hold. Cut yarn and re-join to next st, work in established pat to end of row. Cont in pat on these 23 sts until piece measures 4"/10cm from beg of opening, end with a WS row. Cut yarn, and re-join to 13 sts on hold. Work until even with other side, end with a WS row.

Next row (RS) Cont in pat across all 36 sts. Work until scarf measures 50"/127cm from beg. Bind off. To wear as shown, fold in half lengthwise and pull both ends through keyhole.

MOSAIC SCARF

Rose Callahan

TOOLKIT

YARN
- 3½oz/100g, 220yd/200m of any DK weight wool in light blue (MC) and grey (CC)

NEEDLES
- One pair size 6 (4mm) needles OR SIZE TO OBTAIN GAUGE

MEASUREMENTS
Approximately 8 x 60"/20.5 x152.5cm

GAUGE
19 sts and 32 rows to 4"/10cm over slip st pattern, using size 6 (4mm) needles.
TAKE TIME TO CHECK YOUR GAUGE.

STITCH GLOSSARY
MOSAIC PATTERN
(multiple of 12 sts plus 2)
Row 1 (RS) With MC, knit.
Row 2 With MC, purl.
Row 3 With CC, *sl 2 wyib, k10; rep from * end sl 2 wyib.
Row 4 With CC, sl 2 wyif, *k10, sl 2 wyif; rep from * to end.
Rows 5-8 Rep rows 1-4.
Rows 9 and 10 Rep rows 1 and 2.
Row 11 With CC, *k6, sl 2 wyib, k4; rep from *, end k2.
Row 12 With CC, k2, *k4, sl 2 wyif, k6; rep from * to end.
Rows 13-16 Rep rows 9-14.
Rep rows 1-16 for mosaic pattern.

SCARF
With MC and size 6 (4mm) needles, cast on 38 sts.
BEG MOSAIC PAT
Work in mosaic pat until scarf measures approx 60"/20.5cm from beg. Bind off with MC.

TOOLKIT

YARN ④
- 4⁴/₅oz/150g, 400yd/370m of any worsted weight wool blend

NEEDLES
- One pair size 10 (6mm) needles OR SIZE TO OBTAIN GAUGE

MEASUREMENTS
Approximately 7 x 70"/18 x 177.5cm

GAUGE
17 sts and 21 rows to 4"/10cm over St st using size 10 (6mm) needles.
TAKE TIME TO CHECK GAUGE.

STITCH GLOSSARY
Kfb Inc 1 st by k into front and back of next st.

SCARF
With size 10 (6mm) needles, cast on 48 sts. Knit 4 rows.
Row 1 (RS) Knit.
Row 2 and all WS rows K3, p to last 3 sts, k3.
Row 3 K3, [k3tog] 14 times, k3—20 sts.
Row 5 K3, [kfb] 14 times, k3—34 sts.
Row 7 K3, [kfb, k3] 7 times, k3—41 sts.
Row 9 K3, [kfb, k4] 7 times, k3—48 sts.
Row 10 K3, p to last 3 sts, k3.
Rep rows 1–10 until scarf measures 69"/175cm from beg, end with a row 9.
K 4 rows. Bind off.

Rose Sheifer

CABLED RIB SCARF

MEASUREMENTS

Approximately 7½ x 60"/19 x 152.5cm

GAUGE

20 sts and 16 rows to 4"/10cm over k2, p2 rib (unstretched) using size 10½ (6.5mm) needles.
TAKE TIME TO CHECK YOUR GAUGE.

STITCH GLOSSARY

16-st RC

Slip 8 sts to cn and hold to *back*, [k2, p2] twice, work sts from cn as foll: [k2, p2] twice.

16-st LC

Slip 8 sts to cn and hold to *front*, [k2, p2] twice, work sts from cn as foll: [k2, p2] twice.

SCARF

With size 10½ (6.5mm) needles, cast on 40 sts.
Row 1 *K2, p2; rep from * to end.
Row 2 K the knit sts and p the purl sts.
Rep row 2 for k2, p2 rib for 10 rows more. Work foll chart until 20 rows have been worked 11 times. Work 7 rows more in k2, p2 rib. Bind off in rib.

Chart rows (left side, even): 20, 18, 16, 14, 12, 10, 8, 6, 4, 2
Chart rows (right side, odd): 19, 17, 15, 13, 11, 9, 7, 5, 3, 1

40 sts

STITCH KEY

- ☐ k on RS, p on WS
- — p on RS, k on WS
- 16-st RC
- 16-st LC

CHUNKY SCARF

TOOLKIT

YARN
- 17½oz/500g, 300yd/275m of any super-bulky weight wool

NEEDLES
- One pair size 15 (10mm) needles OR SIZE TO OBTAIN GAUGE

MEASUREMENTS
Approximately 8 x 76"/20.5 x 190.5cm

GAUGE
10 sts and 12 rows to 4"/10cm over pattern st using size 15 (10mm) needles.
TAKE TIME TO CHECK GAUGE.

STITCH GLOSSARY

PATTERN STITCH
(over an even number of sts)
Row 1 (RS) Knit.
Row 2 K1, *k2tog; rep from * to last st, k1.
Row 3 K1, *kfb; rep from * to last st, k1.
Row 4 K1, p to last st, k1.
Row 5 Knit.
Row 6 Rep row 4.
Rows 7–10 Rep rows 1-4.
Rep rows 1-10 for pat st.

SCARF
With size 15 (10mm) needles, cast on 20 sts.
Work in pat st for 75½"/191.5cm or desired length. Bind off.

Paul Amato

WAVES SCARF

Paul Amato

TOOLKIT

YARN ④
- 7oz/200g, 300yd/275m of any worsted weight cotton

NEEDLES
- One size 11 (8mm) circular needle 29"/74cm long OR SIZE TO OBTAIN GAUGE

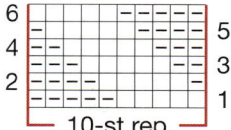

10-st rep

STITCH KEY
☐ k on RS, p on WS
⊟ p on RS, k on WS

MEASUREMENTS
Approximately 7 x 59"/18 x 149.5cm

GAUGE
12 sts and 23 rows to 4"/10cm over chart pat using size 11 (8mm) needles. TAKE TIME TO CHECK GAUGE.

NOTE
Circular needle is used to accommodate large number of sts. Do not join.

SCARF
With size 11 (8mm) needle, cast on 180 sts very loosely. Knit 4 rows.

BEG CHART
Next row (RS) K5, work row 1 of chart, working 10-st rep 17 times, k5. Cont in pats as established, working first and last 5 sts of every row in garter st (k every row) and rem sts in chart pat, until 6 rows of chart have been worked 5 times. Rep rows 1-5 once more.
Knit 4 rows. Bind off very loosely.

BOYFRIEND SCARF

Jack Deutsch

TOOLKIT

YARN

- 10½oz/300g, 600yd/550m of any worsted weight wool in brown (A)
- 3½oz/100g, 240yd/220m in tan (B)

NEEDLES

- Size 5 (3.75mm) circular needle, 40"/100cm long OR SIZE TO OBTAIN GAUGE

MEASUREMENTS

Approx 9 x 96"/23 x 244cm

GAUGE

17 sts and 42 rows to 4"/10cm over garter and dot st stripe pat using size 5 (3.75mm) needles.
TAKE TIME TO CHECK GAUGE.

Note Scarf is knit lengthwise, that is casting on all sts for total length of scarf. For the self-fringe, an end of 7"/18cm is left at beg and end of every row to be fringed later (This will alleviate all ends being sewn in when scarf is finished).

STITCH GLOSSARY

GARTER AND DOT STITCH PATTERN
Leaving a 7"/18cm end of yarn, with circular needle and A, cast on any number of sts. K1 row with A and cut A leaving a 7"/18cm end of yarn.
Row 1 Leaving a 7"/18cm end of yarn, with B, knit. Cut yarn leaving a 7"/18cm end.
Row 2 Leaving a 7"/18cm end of yarn, with A, knit. Cut yarn leaving a 7"/18cm end.
Row 3 Rep row 1.
Rows 4–8 Rep row 2.
Rep rows 1–8 for garter and dot st pattern.

SCARF

With A, cast on 400 sts. Work in 8-row garter and dot st pat for a total of 11 reps of the 8-row pat. Then, work rows 1–4 once more. Bind off knitwise with A.

FINISHING

Block lightly to measurements.
FRINGE
Knot 2 ends of fringe with adjacent 2 ends of fringe. Knot a second time. Trim fringe to 4½"/11.5cm.

TOOLKIT

YARN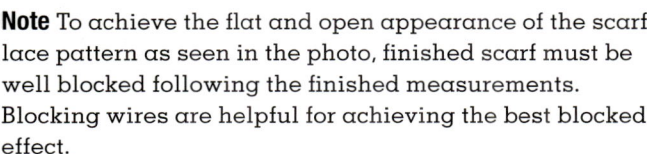
- 1¾oz/50g, 450yd/410m of any lace weight mohair blend

NEEDLES
- One pair size 3 (3.25mm) needles OR SIZE TO OBTAIN GAUGE

OTHER
- Blocking wires

MEASUREMENTS
Approx 11 x 58"/28 x 147cm

GAUGE
21 sts and 30 rows to 4"/10cm over lace pat st (after blocking) foll chart using size 3 (3.25mm) needles.
TAKE TIME TO CHECK GAUGE.

Note To achieve the flat and open appearance of the scarf lace pattern as seen in the photo, finished scarf must be well blocked following the finished measurements. Blocking wires are helpful for achieving the best blocked effect.

SCARF
Cast on 59 sts.
Row 1 (WS) Sl 1 st purlwise, k to end.
Rep row 1 for garter st border for a total of 7 rows.

BEG CHART PATTERN
Row 1 (RS) Working row 1 of chart, work sts 1–6, then work 6-st rep (sts 7–12) 7 times, work sts 13–23. Cont to foll chart in this way, rep rows 1–16 of chart a total of 24 times. Work chart row 1 once more
Next row (WS) Sl 1 st purlwise, k to end. Rep this row 5 times more. Bind off loosely on WS row.

Jack Deutsch Studios

FINISHING
Lay work flat and pin carefully in place, stretching scarf out severely to finished measurements (or use blocking wires). Mist lightly with water, then leave scarf to dry.

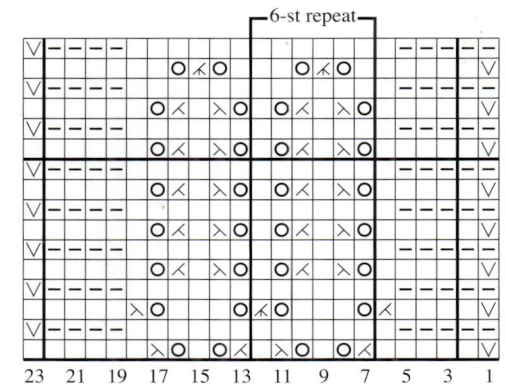

Stitch Key
- ☐ K on RS, p on WS
- ⊟ P on RS, k on WS
- ☑ Sl 1 st purlwise
- K2tog
- Ssk
- K3tog
- ◯ Yo

RIPPLING WAVES SCARF

TOOLKIT

YARN

- 10½oz/300g, 690yd/630m of any DK weight wool blend

NEEDLES

- One pair size 6 (4mm) needles OR SIZE TO OBTAIN GAUGE

MEASUREMENTS

Approx 9 x 60"/ 23 x 152cm

GAUGE

21 sts and 44 rows to 4"/10cm over lace pat st using size 6 (4mm) needles.
TAKE TIME TO CHECK GAUGE.

Notes

1 There is a 3-st seed st border (worked as p1, k1, p1) worked at beg and end of every row along the length of the scarf. To maintain a flat edge to compensate for differing row gauges between the lace pat and these garter st edges, short rows are worked on every pat row 16 as foll: **Row 16** [P1, k1, p1, turn] twice, p1, k1, p1, then work across over the lace body of scarf to last 3 sts, [p1, k1, p1, turn] twice, p1, k1, p1. To maintain a flat edge in this way, no st wrapping is required.
2 All yo's on RS rows are worked as p sts on WS rows.

SCARF

Cast on 48 sts.
Row 1 (RS) P1, k1, p1, *k6, p3; rep from * ending last rep p1, k1, p1 instead of p3.
Row 2 and all WS rows P1, k1, p1, *knit the knit sts and purl the purl sts; rep from * to last 3 sts, p1, k1, p1.
Row 3 P1, k1, p1, *yo, k2, ssk, k2, p3; rep from *, ending last rep p1, k1, p1 instead of p3.
Row 5 P1, k1, p1, *k1, yo, k2, ssk, k1, p3; rep from *, ending last rep p1, k1, p1 instead of p3.
Row 7 P1, k1, p1, *k2, yo, k2, ssk, p3; rep from *, ending last rep p1, k1, p1 instead of p3.
Row 9 Rep row 1.
Row 11 P1, k1, p1, *k2, k2tog, k2, yo, p3; rep from *, ending last rep p1, k1, p1 instead of p3.
Row 13 P1, k1, p1, *k1, k2tog, k2, yo, k1, p3; rep from *, ending last rep p1, k1, p1 instead of p3.
Row 15 P1, k1, p1, *k2tog, k2, yo, k2, p3; rep from *, ending last rep p1, k1, p1 instead of p3.
Row 16 See short row borders note, above.
Rep rows 1–16 for lace pat st until piece measures 60"/152cm from beg. Bind off.

Jack Deutsch Studios

EDGING

Note Edging is worked lengthwise. Slip all the sl sts knitwise.
Cast on 8 sts.
Row 1 *K1, p1; rep from * to end.
Row 2 *P1, k1; rep from * to end.
Row 3 Rep row 1 (for 3 rows in seed st).
Row 4 Sl 1, k2, yo, k2tog, yo twice, k2tog, k1—9 sts.
Row 5 K3, p1, k2, yo, k2tog, k1.
Row 6 Sl 1, k2, yo, k2tog, k1, yo twice, k2tog, k1—10 sts.
Row 7 K3, p1, k3, yo, k2tog, k1.
Row 8 Sl 1, k2, yo, k2tog, k2, yo twice, k2tog, k1—11 sts.
Row 9 K3, p1, k4, yo, k2tog, k1.
Row 10 Sl 1, k2, yo, k2tog, k6.
Row 11 Bind off 3 sts knitwise (1 st rems on RH needle from bind-off), k4, yo, k2tog, k1—8 sts.
Rep rows 4–11 until piece fits lengthwise along one end of scarf, ending with row 10. Bind off 3 sts, p1, [k1, p1] 3 times. Work 1 more row in seed st on 8 sts. Bind off in seed st.

FINISHING

Block scarf to measurements. Sew edging to both ends of scarf.

SERPENTINE TWIST

Jack Deutsch Studios

TOOLKIT

YARN ④

- 1¾oz/50g, 300yd/280m of any worsted weight mohair blend

NEEDLES

- One pair size 6 (4mm) needles OR SIZE TO OBTAIN GAUGE

OTHER

- Cable needle (cn)

MEASUREMENTS

Approx 4 (at widest point) x 73"/11.5 x 185cm

GAUGE

28 sts and 24 rows to 4"/10cm over rib and cable pat using size 6 (4mm) needles.
TAKE TIME TO CHECK GAUGE.

SCARF

Cast on 6 sts.
Row 1 (RS) Sl 1 st purlwise, k2, p2, p last st.
Row 2 Sl 1 st purlwise, M1, k2, p2, p last st—7 sts.
Row 3 Sl 1 st purlwise, M1, k2, p2, k1, p last st—8 sts.
Row 4 Sl 1 st purlwise, M1, p1, k2, p2, k1, p last st—9 sts.
Cont to work in this way, working M1 at beg of every row

after first sl st and p last st of every row, adding inc'd sts in k2, p2 rib until there are 32 sts (23 rows more).
Work 1 row even in k2, p2 rib as established. *
Next (cable) row (RS) Sl 16 sts to cn and hold to back, work next 16 sts in rib, work 16 sts from holder in rib.
Work even for 29 rows*. Rep between *'s 12 times more.
Rep cable row once more.
Next (dec) row Sl 1 st purlwise, work 2 sts in rib, pass the 2nd st on RH needle over the first st (for dec 1 st), work rib to last st, p1. Rep this row 25 times more—6 sts rem. Bind off in rib.

FINISHING

Block scarf lightly to measurements. If desired, tack scarf at cabled crossing points on WS so that cabled edges lie flat instead of twisting.

TOOLKIT

YARN

-  5¼oz/150g, 525yd/480m of any worsted weight wool in light green (A)
- 1¾oz/50g, 175yd/160m of a worsted weight wool in both plum (C) and pink (E)
- 1¾oz/50g, 195yd/175m of a fingering weight wool in soft violet (D)
- .88oz/25g, 229yd/210m of a DK weight mohair blend in orchid (D)
- 1¾oz/50g, 125yd/115m of DK weight wool and cotton blend in both olive (F) and lt olive (G)

NEEDLES

- One pair each size 4 and 6 (3.5 and 4mm) needles OR SIZE TO OBTAIN GAUGE

OTHER

- Cable needle (cn)

MEASUREMENTS

Approx 7¼ x 39½"/18.5 x 100cm

GAUGE

36 sts and 34 rows to 4"/10cm over pat foll chart using size 6 (4mm) needles. TAKE TIME TO CHECK GAUGE.

STITCH GLOSSARY

4-st RC
Sl next 2 sts to cn and hold to back, k2, k2 from cn.
4-st LC
Sl next 2 sts to cn and hold to front, k2, k2 from cn
BOBBLE (in F or G)
Worked in st designated on chart, work 4 rows as foll:
Row 1 (RS) K1, p1, k1 into one st, turn.
Row 2 K3, turn.
Row 3 P3, turn.
Row 4 K3tog, turn.

Note When working with A, C, E, F and G, use 1 strand. When working with B, use 2 strands held together. When working with D, use 3 strands held together.

SCARF

With smaller needles and A, cast on 64 sts. K4 rows. Change to larger needles. Work in cable and color foll chart until 12 reps of 28-row rep of chart have been completed. Piece measures approx 39¼"/99.5cm from beg. Change to smaller needles. With A, k3 rows. Bind off knitwise.

FINISHING

Block scarf to measurements.

KNOTTED FRINGE

Using B, cut 24"/61cm lengths using 4 lengths for each of the 9 fringe at each end of scarf. Knot each of the 9 fringe at the lower edge. Then take 4 strands from one fringe and combine with 4 strands of next fringe at approx ½"/1.5cm from first row of knots. Alternating as in photo, make 3 more rows of knots. Trim evenly.

Stitch and Color Key

☐ K on RS, p on WS	☐ Lt green (A)
⊟ P on RS, k on WS	☐ Soft violet (B) 2 Strands
⧑ 4-ST RC	☐ Plum (C)
⧑ 4-ST LC	☐ Orchid (D) 3 Strands
● Bobble in Olive (F)	☐ Pink (E)
● Bobble in Lt. olive (G)	☐ Olive (F)
	☐ Lt olive (G)

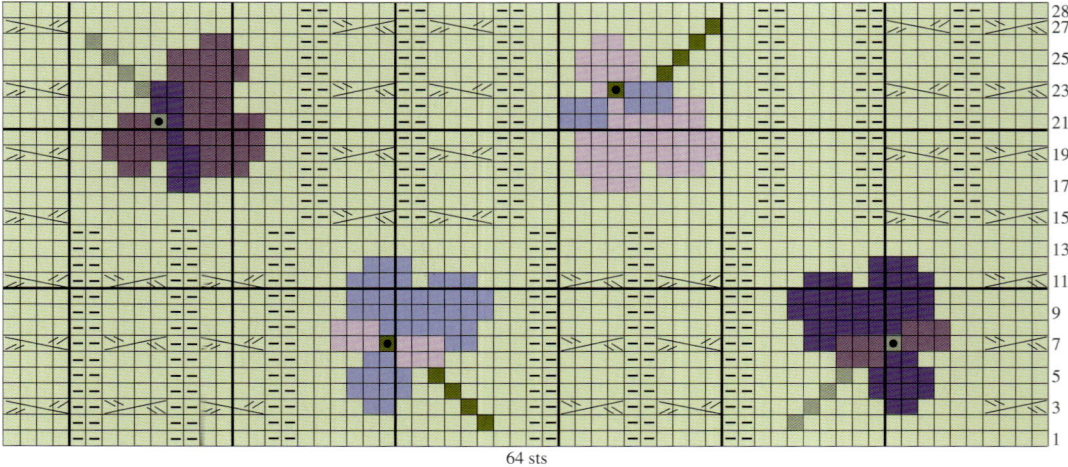

64 sts

FANCIFUL SCARF

TOOLKIT

YARN (4)
Use a mix of yarns totaling 323–369yd/315–360m in shades of blue and green in the following types:
- (A) green and blue variegated worsted weight textured yarn
- (B) multi-color worsted weight rayon and cotton slub (unevenly spun) yarn
- (C) worsted weight, chenille yarn
- (D) worsted weight metallic yarn
- (E) fine, worsted weight eyelash yarn

NEEDLES
- One pair size 7 (4.5mm) needles OR SIZE TO OBTAIN GAUGE
- Size 7 (4.5mm) circular needle, 29"/74cm long

OTHER
- Size H/8 (5mm) crochet hook

Jack Deutsch

MEASUREMENTS
Approx 5 x 50"/12.5 x 127cm

GAUGE
16 sts and 42 rows to 4"/10cm over welt pat st using a variety of yarns and size 7 (4.5mm) needles.
TAKE TIME TO CHECK GAUGE.

NOTE
To create the scarf as in the photo, a new color and type of yarn is worked in each row leaving yarn at both ends to create the fringe. The length of the fringe is as desired. When using the finer weight, yarn may need to be doubled to achieve the right look.

STITCH GLOSSARY
WELT PATTERN STITCH
Rows 1, 2 and 3 Knit.
Row 4 Purl.
Rep these 4 rows for welt pat st.

SCARF
Leaving approx 10"/25.5cm for fringe, with desired yarn and crochet hook, chain approx 200 sts, leaving 10"/25.5 cm for opposite fringe. Being sure that chain is fairly loose, pick up and k 1 st in each ch (for chain cast-on). With circular needle, knit 1 row. Cut yarn with fringe end. Leaving 10"/25.5 cm for fringe (and knot each new yarn using a single knot method), cont to work the 4-row welt pat st, changing to a new yarn on each row and cont in this way until 36 rows in welt pat st are completed. Bind off loosely (being sure that edge is as flexible as the cast-on edge).

FINISHING
Block lightly. Make a large overhand knot at each end. Trim fringe to a tapered point, if desired.

FUR TRIMMED SCARF

TOOLKIT

YARN
- ② 3½oz/100g, 560yd/510 m of any sport weight wool blend in cream (A)
- ⑤ 1¾oz/50g, 60yd/50m of any bulky weight "fun fur" yarn in tan (B)

NEEDLES
- One pair size 5 (3.5mm) needles OR SIZE TO OBTAIN GAUGE

OTHER
- One each sizes E/4 (3.5mm) and G/6 (4.5mm) crochet hooks

Jack Deutsch

MEASUREMENTS
Approx 10½ x 35"/26.5 x 89cm.

GAUGE
19 sts and 35 rows to 4"/10cm over seed st using 2 strands of yarn held tog and size 5 (3.5mm) needles.
TAKE TIME TO CHECK GAUGE.

NOTE
Work with 2 strands of yarn held tog throughout.

STITCH GLOSSARY
SEED STITCH PATTERN
(over an odd number of sts)
Row 1 (RS) K1, *p1, k1; rep from * to end.
Rep row 1 for seed st pat. This stitch is reversible.

SCARF
With 2 strands of A and size 5 (3.5mm) needles, cast on 51 sts. Work in seed st pat for 8"/20.5cm.

SLIT OPENING
Next row (RS) Work 18 sts in seed st, bind off center 15 sts for slit, work 18 sts in seed st.
Next row (WS) Work in seed st to center bound-off sts, with 2 strands of A, cast on 16 sts over these sts, then pass next st on LH needle over the last cast-on st (for a neat edge of opening), work in seed st to end. Cont in seed st on all 51 sts until scarf measures 35"/89cm from beg. Bind off.

FINISHING
Block very lightly to measurements.

FUR TRIM EDGE
Row 1 (RS) With 1 strand A, and size E/4 (3.5mm) hook, work 1 sc in each st along one short end of scarf. Fasten off A.
Row 2 (RS) Join B to work row from RS, and with size G (4.5mm) hook, work 1 sc in each sc across. Fasten off B tightly. Cut end to approx 1"/2.5cm long to blend in with the fur edge (it is easier to cut the end instead of weaving it in which will cause extra bulk).

Jack Deutsch

MEASUREMENTS
Approx 11½ x 60"/29 x 152cm

GAUGE
24 sts and 32 rows to 4"/10cm over pat st using size 6 (4mm) needles.
TAKE TIME TO CHECK GAUGE.

STITCH GLOSSARY
PATTERN STITCH
(over an even number of sts)
Row 1 (RS) K1, *yo k2tog; rep from *, end k1.
Rep this row for pat st.

Note Due to the ability of this pattern stitch to stretch and lightweight yarn, the finished measurements should be determined by laying piece flat and pulling scarf in shape both widthwise and lengthwise.

SCARF
Cast on 68 sts loosely. Work in pat st until piece measures 60"/152cm from beg. Bind off loosely.

FINISHING
Block scarf to finished measurements.

FRINGE
Cut a piece of cardboard to 9"/23cm on one side. Using this piece of cardboard, wind yarn 8–10 times around for each individual fringe. Cut one end of strands to form fringe. Slide crochet hook into space (from WS) at end of scarf and pull through looped end of fringe. Tighten to form a knot. Place 17 fringe at each end of scarf. Trim ends of fringe neatly.

PATCHWORK SCARF

TOOLKIT

YARN

- 3½oz/100g, 220yd/200m of any worsted weight wool blend in blue (A), purple (B) and green (C)

NEEDLES

- One pair size 8 (5mm) needles OR SIZE TO OBTAIN GAUGE

MEASUREMENTS

Approx 8 x 66"/20.5 x 168cm

GAUGE

18 sts and 32 rows to 4"/10cm over garter st using size 8 (5mm) needles.
TAKE TIME TO CHECK GAUGE.

STITCH GLOSSARY

K1 below

K1 st into the st directly one row below. The original stitch will sit ontop of the new stitch made.

Notes

1 For easier working, wind small balls of yarn for each block of color for completing a row of blocks. Twist yarns tog when changing colors.
2 Foll diagram as a guide for the color placement of entire scarf.

SCARF

With A, cast on 13 sts; then cont with B, cast on 13 sts; then cont with C, cast on 13 sts—39 sts total.

BEG PATCHWORK PATTERN

Row 1 (RS) With C, k13; with B, k13; with A, k13.
Row 2 With A, [p1, k1 below] 6 times, p1; with B, [p1, k1 below] 6 times, p1; with C, k13.
Rows 3–24 Rep rows 1 and 2 11 times more.
Row 25 (RS) With A, k13; with C, k13; with B, k13.
Row 26 With B, [p1, k1 below] 6 times, p1; with C, k13; with A, [p1, k1 below] 6 times, p1.
Rows 27–48 Rep rows 25 and 26 11 times more.
Row 49 (RS) With B, k13; with A, k13; with C, k13.
Row 50 With C, k13; with A, [p1, k1 below] 6 times, p1; with B, [p1, k1 below] 6 times, p1.
Rows 51–72 Rep rows 49 and 50 11 times more.
Rep these 72 rows a total of 7 times (see chart). Then, work rows 1–24 once more. Bind off all sts.

Jack Deutsch

FINISHING

Block very lightly (although blocking may be unnecessary due to the nature of the st patterns).

FRINGE

Cut A, B and C into 12"/30.5cm lengths. Taking 4 strands tog for each fringe and folding in half, work 6 fringe in each square matching colors of scarf squares.

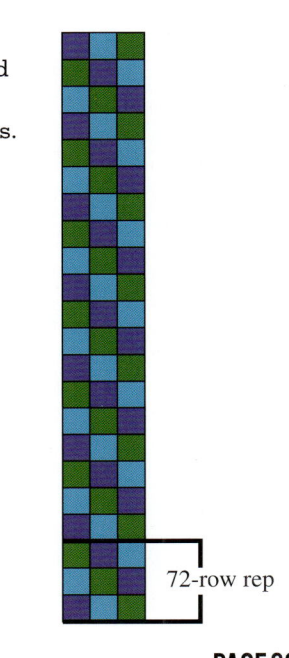

Color Key

- ■ Blue (A) squares in rib
- ■ Purple (B) squares in rib
- ■ Green (C) squares in garter st

72-row rep

MEASUREMENTS
Approx 6"/15cm wide and 52"/132cm long at longest point and 39"/99cm long at shortest point.

GAUGE
20 sts and 40 rows to 4"/10cm over garter st using size 7 (4.5mm) needles.
One triangle measures 13"/33cm at widest point and 6"/15cm high at center.
TAKE TIME TO CHECK GAUGE.

TOOLKIT

YARN
- 3½oz/100g, 260yd/230m of any worsted weight wool in black (A), rust (B), gold (C), white (D), dark pink (E), pink (F), and berry pink (G)

NEEDLES
- One pair size 7 (4.5mm) needles OR SIZE TO OBTAIN GAUGE

Note Work colors as designated for each triangle or in a random striping pattern as desired.

BASE TRIANGLE
With designated color, cast on 89 sts.
Row 1 (RS) K43, k3tog, k43—87 sts.
Row 2 Knit.
Row 3 K2tog, k40, k3tog, k40, k2tog—83 sts.
Row 4 Knit.
Row 5 K2tog, k38, k3tog, k38, k2tog—79 sts.
Row 6 Knit.
Row 7 K2tog, k36, k3tog, k36, k2tog—75 sts.
Row 8 Knit. Cont to dec in this way working a k2tog at beg and end of every other row and a k3tog at center of this row until 7 sts rem and 42 rows have been worked.
Row 43 K2tog, k3tog, k2tog—3 sts.
Row 44 Knit.
Row 45 K3tog and fasten off.

SCARF
Work 7 triangles foll pattern of base triangle and layout foll diagram.

TRIANGLE 1
Work 2 rows black (A), 6 rows rust (B), 4 rows gold (C), 2 rows black (A), 2 rows white (D), 4 rows dk pink (E), 6 rows pink (F), 2 rows black (A), 4 rows berry (G), 2 rows white (D), 2 rows dk pink (E), 6 rows gold (C), 3 rows black (A).

TRIANGLE 2
Work 2 rows berry (G), 2 rows white (D), 6 rows gold (C), 2 rows black (A), 4 rows dk pink (E), 2 rows white (D), 6 rows rust (B), 4 rows pink (F), 2 rows black (A), 2 rows dk pink (E), 6 rows berry (G), 4 rows gold (C), 3 rows black (A).

TRIANGLE 3
Work 2 rows white (D), 2 rows black (A), 6 rows pink (F), 4 rows dk pink (E), 2 rows berry (G), 2 rows white (D), 6 rows rust (B), 2 rows gold (C), 2 rows black (A), 4 rows gold (C), 2 rows white (D), 4 rows dk pink (E), 4 rows berry (G), 3 rows black (A).

TRIANGLE 4
Work 2 rows black (A), 6 rows pink (F), 4 rows dk pink (E), 2 rows white (D), 2 rows black (A), 2 rows gold (C), 2 rows black (A), 6 rows berry (G), 2 rows white (D), 2 rows black (A), 4 rows gold (C), 4 rows rust (B), 2 rows white (D), 2 rows dk pink (E), 3 rows black (A).

TRIANGLE 5
Work 2 rows gold (C), 6 rows berry (G), 2 rows white (D), 2 rows black (A), 6 rows dk pink (E), 2 rows pink (F), 2 rows berry (G), 4 rows pink (F), 2 rows black (A), 2 rows white (D), 4 rows rust (B), 2 rows gold (C), 2 rows berry (G), 4 rows pink (F), 3 rows black (A).

TRIANGLE 6
Work 2 rows black (A), 4 rows dk pink (E), 2 rows white (D), 6 rows berry (G), 4 rows gold (C), 2 rows black (A), 2 rows pink (F), 4 rows dk pink (E), 2 rows white (D), 6 rows rust (B), 2 rows black (A), 2 rows white (D), 4 rows gold (C), 3 rows black (A).

TRIANGLE 7
Work 2 rows dk pink (E), 2 rows black (A), 6 rows pink (F), 2 rows berry (G), 2 rows white (D), 2 rows dk pink (E), 4 rows gold (C), 2 rows black (A), 2 rows white (D), 6 rows rust (B), 2 rows white (D), 4 rows dk pink (E), 2 rows black (A), 2 rows gold (C), 2 rows berry (G), 3 rows black (A).

FINISHING
Block pieces lightly to measurements. Layout foll diagram. Sew each triangle tog forming scarf by using overcast st and matching colors.

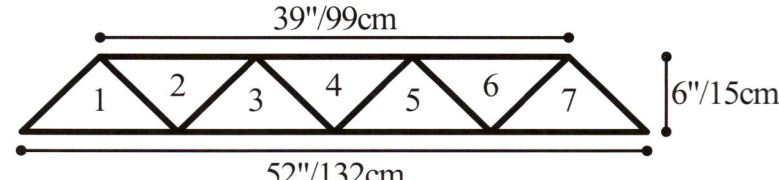

MEASUREMENTS

9 x 56"/23 x 142cm (without fringe)

GAUGE

20 sts and 24 rows to 4"/10cm over backround pat using size 9 (5.5mm) needles.
TAKE TIME TO CHECK GAUGE.

STITCH GLOSSARY

RIGHT TWIST (RT) K2tog leaving sts on LH needle, insert RH needle between the 2 sts just worked and k the first st again, sl both sts from needle tog.
Note When working two-color cables, always match the colors from the previous row.
4-St RC Sl 2 sts to cn and hold to *back*, k2, k2 from cn.
4-St LC Sl 2 sts to cn and hold to *front*, k2, k2 from cn.
5-St RC Sl 3 sts to cn and hold to *back*, k2, sl center st from cn back to LH needle and knit it, k2 from cn.

SCARF

With A, cast on 46 sts.
Row 1 (RS) *K2tog, yo; rep from * to last 2 sts, k2tog—45 sts.
Row 2 *K1, p1; rep from * to end.
BEG CHART 1
Work in St st, beg with row 1 and work 9-st color rep 5 times. Cont as established through chart row 11. Change to A.
Next row (WS) Purl. **Next row (RS)** *K2tog, yo; rep from * end k1. P 1 row.
BEG CHART 2
Work rows 1-16 of chart in colors as indicated, rep rows 1-16 until piece measures 53"/134.5cm from beg, end with a RS row. Change to A.
Next row (WS) Purl.
Next row (RS) K1, yo, *k2tog, yo; rep from * end k1. P 1 row.
BEG CHART 1
Work in St st, beg with row 1 and work 9-st color rep 5 times. Cont as established through chart row 11. Change to A.
Next row (WS) Purl
Next row (RS) *K1, p1; rep from * to end.
Next row (WS) *P2tog, yo; rep from *, end p1—46 sts.
Bind off.

FINISHING
FRINGE
With A, B and C, cut 5"/12.5cm lengths. Using the holes made on edges of scarf, tie fringe using 3 strands; 2 of A and 1 of either B or C, alternating each fringe.

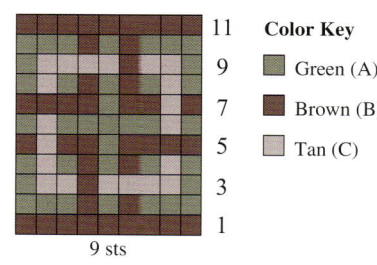

9 sts

Color Key
- Green (A)
- Brown (B)
- Tan (C)

Stitch Key

Note: Work all sts matching colors as shown

- K on RS, p on WS
- P on RS, k on WS
- Yo
- K2tog
- SSK
- RT
- 4-st RC
- 4-st LC
- 5-st RC

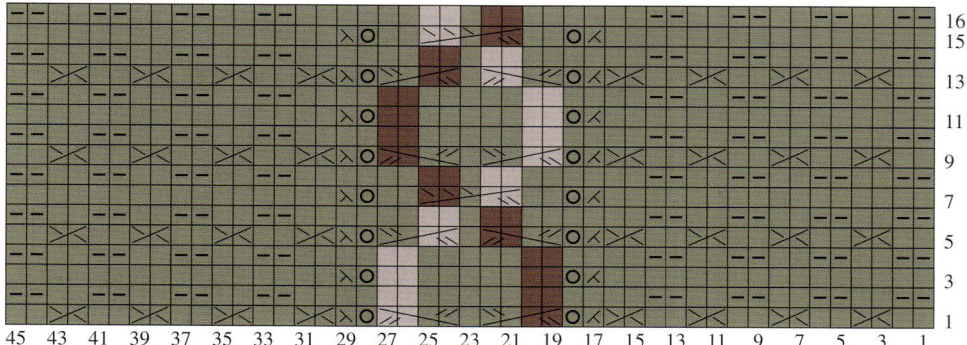

BELL PATTERN SCARF

Quenet

TOOLKIT

YARN
- 17½oz/500g, 300yd/275m of any super-bulky weight wool

NEEDLES
- One pair size 15 (10mm) needles OR SIZE TO OBTAIN GAUGE

OTHER
- Stitch holders

MEASUREMENTS
Approx 11½ x 52"/29 x 132cm

GAUGE
8 sts and 14 rows to 4"/10cm over pat st using size 15 (10mm) needles.
TAKE TIME TO CHECK GAUGE.

STITCH GLOSSARY
PATTERN STITCH (multiple of 9 sts plus 5)
Note St count varies on each row. Count sts after row 8 only.
Row 1 (RS) K3, *yo, k8, yo, k1; rep from * to last 2 sts, k2.
Row 2 K4, *p8, k3 rep from * to last st, k1.
Row 3 K4, *yo, k8 yo, k3; rep from * to last st, k1.
Row 4 K5, *p8, k5 rep from * to end.
Row 5 K5, *yo, k8 yo, k5; rep from * to end.

Row 6 K6, *p8, k7; rep from *, end k6.
Row 7 K6, *k4tog tbl, k4tog, k7; rep from *, end k6.
Row 8 Knit.
Rep rows 1–8 for pat st.

NOTE
Scarf is worked in two pieces then joined together at the center.

SCARF
Cast on 23 sts.
FIRST PIECE
Work 8 rows of pat st 11 times. Place sts on holder. Work 2nd piece same as first.

FINISHING
Block pieces to measurements.
With RS facing, work 3-needle bind-off to join the two pieces (see page 8).

TOOLKIT

YARN (4)

- 10½oz/300g, 385yd/355m of any worsted weight wool blend in dark blue (MC)
- 3½oz/100g, 130yd/120m in light blue (A)

NEEDLES

- One pair size 9 (5.5mm) needles OR SIZE TO OBTAIN GAUGE

OTHER

- Size F/5 (3.75mm) crochet hook

Quenet

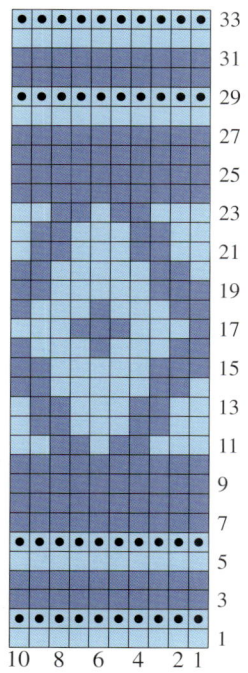

Color and Stitch Key

- K on RS, p on WS with A
- K on RS, p on WS with MC
- K on WS with A

MEASUREMENTS

Approx 8½ x 75"/21.5 x 190.5cm

GAUGE

16 sts and 21 rows to 4"/10cm over St st using size 9 (5.5mm) needles.
TAKE TIME TO CHECK GAUGE.

SCARF

With MC, cast on 31 sts. Work in St st for 4 rows. Cont in St st (except as noted on chart) as work as foll:

BEG CHART

[Work 10-st rep of chart 3 times, then work first st once more. Cont as established, through chart row 33. Cont in St st and MC for 4"/10cm, end with a WS row] twice. Work 32 rows of chart. Cont in St st and MC for 18"/45.5cm. Rep from * to * once. Cont in St st and MC for 4 rows. Bind off.

FINISHING

Block to measurements.

FRINGE

Cut 8"/20.5cm strands of A. With crochet hook, attach 1 strand in each st along edges of scarf.

LACY CABLES SCARF

TOOLKIT

YARN (5)
- 3½oz/100g, 190yd/175m of any bulky weight variegated mohair blend

NEEDLES
- One pair size 10½ (6.5mm) needles OR SIZE TO OBTAIN GAUGE

OTHER
- Cable needle (cn)

Quenet

MEASUREMENTS
Approx 9½ x 64"/24 x 162.5cm

GAUGE
12 sts and 16 rows to 4"/10cm over lace and cable pat using size 10½ (6.5mm) needles. TAKE TIME TO CHECK GAUGE.

STITCH GLOSSARY
6-ST LC
Sl 3 sts to cn and hold to *front*, k3, k3 from cn
S2KP
Slip 2 sts tog, k1, pass 2 sl sts over k1
LACE AND CABLE PATTERN
Row 1 (RS) Sl 1, p1, yo, S2KP, yo, p1, k1, [yo, k2tog] twice, 6-st LC, [yo, k2tog] twice, k1, p1, yo, S2KP, yo, p1, k1.
Row 2 and all WS rows Sl 1, k1, p3, k1, p16, k1, p3, k2.
Rows 3 and 11 Sl 1, p1, k3, p1, k1, [k2tog, yo] twice, k6, [k2tog, yo] twice, k1, p1, k3, p1, k1.
Rows 5 and 9 Sl 1, p1, k3, p1, k1, [yo, k2tog] twice, k6, [yo, k2tog] twice, k1, p1, k3, p1, k1.
Row 7 Sl 1, p1, yo, S2KP, yo, p1, k1, [k2tog, yo] twice, 6-st LC, [k2tog, yo] twice, k1, p1, yo, S2KP, yo, p1, k1.
Row 12 Rep row 2.
Rep rows 1–12 for lace and cable pat.

NOTE
Sl sts knitwise when working S2KP in rows 1 and 7 of lace and cable pat. On all other rows, sl st purlwise.

SCARF
Cast on 28 sts loosely.
Preparation row 1 (RS) K1, p1, k3, p1, k16, p1, k3, p1, k1.
Preparation row 2 Sl 1, k1, p3, k1, p16, k1, p3, k2.
Work in lace and cable pat until piece measures 64"/162.5cm, end with a RS row. Bind off loosely.

FINISHING
Block lightly to measurements.

TOOLKIT

YARN

- 8oz/250yd, 260yd/240m of any heavy worsted weight mohair blend in black (A) and white (B)

NEEDLES

- One pair size 10 (6mm) needles OR SIZE TO OBTAIN GAUGE

MEASUREMENTS

Approx 7 x 92"/18 x 233.5cm

GAUGE

14 sts and 24 rows to 4"/10cm over seed st using size 10 (6mm) needles. TAKE TIME TO CHECK GAUGE.

STITCH GLOSSARY

SEED STITCH
(over an even number of sts)
Row 1 (RS) *K1, p1; rep from * to end.
Row 2 K the purl sts and p the knit sts.
Rep row 2 for seed st.

SCARF

With A, cast on 28 sts. *Work in seed st for 18 rows.
Next row (RS) Bind off 7 sts. Cut yarn and join B. Work to end, cast on 7 sts. Rep from * 20 times more, alternating A and B (21 color blocks). Bind off.

Quenet

WOVEN SCARF

TOOLKIT

YARN (4)

- 7oz/200g, 270yd/245m of any heavy worsted weight wool blend in medium blue (MC)
- 3½oz/100g, 135yd/125m in navy (A), rust (B) and light blue (C)

NEEDLES

- One pair size 10½ (6.5mm) needles OR SIZE TO OBTAIN GAUGE

OTHER

- Foam core board
- Quilting pins
- Tapestry needle

MEASUREMENTS

Approx 6 x 67"/15 x 170cm (with fringe)

GAUGE

13 sts and 22 rows to 4"/10cm over seed st using size 10½ (6.5mm) needles.
TAKE TIME TO CHECK GAUGE.

STITCH GLOSSARY

WEAVING PATTERN
With A, weave 1 strand over and under 1 ladder at a time. Rep 3 times more.
With MC, weave 2 strands together over and under 2 ladders at a time.
With B, weave 2 strands together over and under 2 ladders at a time.
With MC, weave 2 strands together over and under 2 ladders at a time.
*With C, weave 3 strands together over and under 3 ladders at a time. Rep from * twice more.
With MC, weave 2 strands together over and under 2 ladders at a time.
With B, weave 2 strands together over and under 2 ladders at a time.
With MC, weave 2 strands together over and under 2 ladders at a time.
With A, weave 1 strand over and under 1 ladder at a time. Rep 3 times more.

SCARF

With MC, cast on 10 sts.
Row 1 (RS) K1, p1, k6, p1, k1.
Row 2 K1, p1, k1, p4, k1, p1, k1. Rep last 2 rows until piece measures 60"/152cm from beg. You will be creating a St st channel with seed st on either side.

Note The scarf will appear narrow and distorted until you drop sts and weave.

BIND OFF ROW

Bind off 2 sts. With 1 st on RH needle, drop the 4 sts in St st and unravel all the way to and through the bind off sts. Elongate the st on the RH needle to bridge the gap created by the dropped sts (approx 4–5"/10–12cm long). Take the tension off the carrying yarn and bind off the elongated st without tightening the st or the carrying yarn. The bind off across the dropped sts must be the same width as the dropped st channel. Cont to bind off all rem sts.

KNIT WEAVING

Cut lengths of yarn for weaving 20"/51cm longer than scarf, as foll: 8 strands A, 4 strands B, 9 strands C, 8 strands MC.
Pin the scarf along each edge of the dropped st channel onto foam core boards (the entire length of the scarf must be pinned from one end to the other). Place pins about 1"/2.5cm apart to keep the channel taut.
Foll weaving pat, using a tapestry needle to weave the cut strands under and over the ladders. Pull the yarn through from one end to the other, leaving tails approx same length at each end. Tug the yarns to the side after weaving each one (a pick comb or tip of knitting needle work well).

FRINGE

Remove the scarf from the foam core and adjust the tension of the weaving yarns as needed. Beg at outside edges and working into center, knot 4 strands of weaving yarn tails at a time with overhead knots. Knot the remaining 5 center strands into one knot. Rep for the other end. For outer edge fringe, cut 16 lengths of MC, 20"/51cm long. Pull 2 strands at a time half way through an edge st and knot into an overhand knot. Add a total of 4 fringe knots on each end, tying in the cast-on and bound-off tails with the edge knots. Trim all fringe to 7"/18cm long.

Quenet

TOOLKIT

YARN (5)
- 14oz/400g, 440yd/400m of any super-bulky weight variegated wool

NEEDLES
- One pair size 11 (8mm) needles OR SIZE TO OBTAIN GAUGE

MEASUREMENTS
Approx 6½ x 68"/16.5 x 172.5cm

GAUGE
12 sts and 15 rows to 4"/10cm over k2, p2 rib (slightly stretched) using size 11 (8mm) needles. TAKE TIME TO CHECK GAUGE.

STITCH GLOSSARY
L-inc
With tip of LH needle, lift and k the left loop of the st below the st just knit on RH needle.
R-inc
With tip of RH needle, lift and k the right loop of the st below the st just knit on LH needle.

SCARF
Cast on 90 sts. Work in rib as foll:
Row 1 (WS) *P6, k6; rep from *, end p6.
Row 2 *K6, p6; rep from *, end k6.
Rep last 2 rows 3 times more, then work row 1 once more.
Next (dec) row (RS) *Ssk, k2, k2tog, p6; rep from * to last 6 sts, ssk, k2, k2tog—74 sts.
Next (dec) row (WS) *P4, ssk, k2, k2tog; rep from *, end p4—60 sts. Work even in k4, p4 rib for 8 rows more.
Next (dec) row (RS) *Ssk, k2tog, p4; rep from * to last 4 sts, ssk, k2tog—44 sts.
Next (dec) row (WS) *P2, ssk, k2tog; rep from *, end p2—30 sts.

Next row (RS) *K2, p2; rep from *, end k2. Work even in k2, p2 rib until piece measures 62"/157.5cm from beg, end with a WS row.
Next (inc ruffle) row (RS) *K1, L-inc, R-inc, k1, p2; rep from *, end k1, L-inc, R-inc, k1—46 sts.
Next (inc ruffle) row (WS) *P4, k1, L-inc, R-inc, k1; rep from *, end p4—60 sts. Work even in k4, p4 rib for 8 rows more
Next (inc) row (RS) *K1, L-inc, k2, R-inc, k1, p4; rep from *, end k1, L-inc, k2, R-inc, k1— 76 sts.
Next (inc) row (WS) *P6, k1, L-inc, k2, R-inc, k1; rep from *, end p6— 90 sts. Work even in k6, p6 rib for 8 rows more. Bind off in pat.

SIMPLE STRIPES SCARF

TOOLKIT

YARN (5)

- 5¼oz/150g, 180yd/165m of any bulky weight wool and acrylic blend in red (MC)

- 1¾oz/50g, 60yd/54m in grey (A) and black (B)

NEEDLES

- Size 10½ (6.5mm) circular needle 32"/80cm OR SIZE TO OBTAIN GAUGE

MEASUREMENTS

Approx 6 x 62"/15 x 157.5cm

GAUGE

12 sts and 20 rows to 4"/10cm over garter st using size 10½ (6.5mm) needles.
TAKE TIME TO CHECK GAUGE.

Notes

1 Scarf is worked horizontally.
2 Circular needle is used to accommodate the large number of sts. Work back and forth in rows.

SCARF

With MC, cast on 180 sts. Work in garter st and stripe pat as foll: work 10 rows MC, 4 rows A, 2 rows B, 4 rows A, 10 rows MC. Bind off in MC.

FELTED CELESTIAL SCARF

Jack Deutsch

TOOLKIT

YARN ④

- 5¼oz/150g, 320yd/290m of any worsted weight wool in royal blue (MC)
- Small amounts each in gold (A) and green (B)

NEEDLES

- One pair size 10½ (6.5mm) needles OR SIZE TO OBTAIN GAUGE

OTHER

- Tapestry needle

Stitch Key

🟡 French knot with A

¾" straight st with B

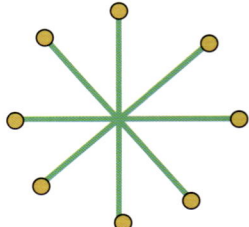

MEASUREMENTS

9¼"/23.5cm wide and 58"/147cm long before felting
5"/13cm wide and 42"/107cm long after felting

GAUGE

13 sts and 18 rows to 4"/10cm over St st (before felting).
TAKE TIME TO CHECK GAUGE

SCARF

With MC, cast on 30 sts. Work in St st until piece measures 58"/147cm.
Bind off.

FELTING

Put scarf in washing machine set to hot wash/cold rinse with low water level. Add one tablespoon dishwashing detergent and ¼ cup baking soda at beginning of wash cycle. Repeat the cycle, if necessary, until piece is felted smooth. Squeeze out excess water and pin flat to dry.

FINISHING

If needed, press gently using steam.
Mark for a slit approximately 4"/10cm long down the center of the scarf starting approx 6"/15cm down from bind-off edge. Cut slit using sharp scissors. With photo as guide, follow diagram and work embroidery using B for spokes and A for French knots.

LUREX EVENING SCARF

Jack Deutsch

MEASUREMENTS
Approx 9 x 47"/24 x 119cm

GAUGE
32 sts and 42 rows to 4"/10cm over ripple pat st using size 3 (3.25mm) needles.
TAKE TIME TO CHECK GAUGE.

STITCH GLOSSARY
RIPPLE PATTERN STITCH (multiple of 11 sts)
Rows 1–5 With A, knit.
Row 6 (RS) With B, *k2tog, k2, inc 1 st in each of next 2 sts (by k into front and back of each st), k3, SKP; rep from * to end.
Row 7 With B, knit.
Rows 8 and 10 Rep row 6.
Rows 9 and 11 With B, purl.
Row 12 With A, rep row 6.
Rep rows 1–12 for ripple pat st.

TOOLKIT
YARN ❶
- 2³/₅oz/75g, 310yd/285m of any fingering weight sparkly acrylic in brown (A)
- .88oz/25g, 102yd/95m in aqua (B), purple (C), grey (D), red (E), and pink (F)

NEEDLES
- One pair size 3 (3.25mm) needles OR SIZE TO OBTAIN GAUGE

SCARF
With A, cast on 77 sts. Foll ripple pat st, rep rows 1–12 and replacing colors in rows 6–11 with C, then D, E and F for a total of 60 rows in color stripe pat.
Note Do not carry colors along side edge of work. Cut colors at end of each color stripe.
Work in this way until 8 reps of 12-row stripe pat are completed and scarf measures approx 46½"/118cm. Then with A, k 4 rows. Bind off knitwise with A.

FINISHING
Sew in all ends neatly on WS of scarf. Block scarf to measurements.

TOOLKIT

YARN (4)

- 7oz/200g, 330yd/305m of any worsted weight wool

NEEDLES

- One pair size 9 (5.5mm) needles OR SIZE TO OBTAIN GAUGE

OTHER

- Cable needle (cn)

KNITTED MEASUREMENTS

Approx 7 x 53"/18 x 134.5cm

GAUGE

24 sts and 22 rows to 4"/10cm over rib and cable pat foll chart using size 9 (5.5mm) needles. TAKE TIME TO CHECK GAUGE.

STITCH GLOSSARY

4-ST RPC

Sl next st to cn and hold to *back*, k next 3 sts, p1 from cn.

4-ST LPC

Sl next 3 sts to cn and hold to *front*, p next st, k3 from cn.

6-ST RC

Sl next 3 sts to cn and hold to *back*, k next 3 sts, k3 from cn.

6-ST LC

Sl next 3 sts to cn and hold to *front*, k next 3 sts, k3 from cn.

SCARF

Cast on 42 sts. Beg with row 1, foll chart through row 6. Then rep rows 7-42 (36-row repeat) a total of 8 times. Then work rows 43-51 once. Bind off in rib.

FINISHING

Block to measurements being sure not to flatten rib.

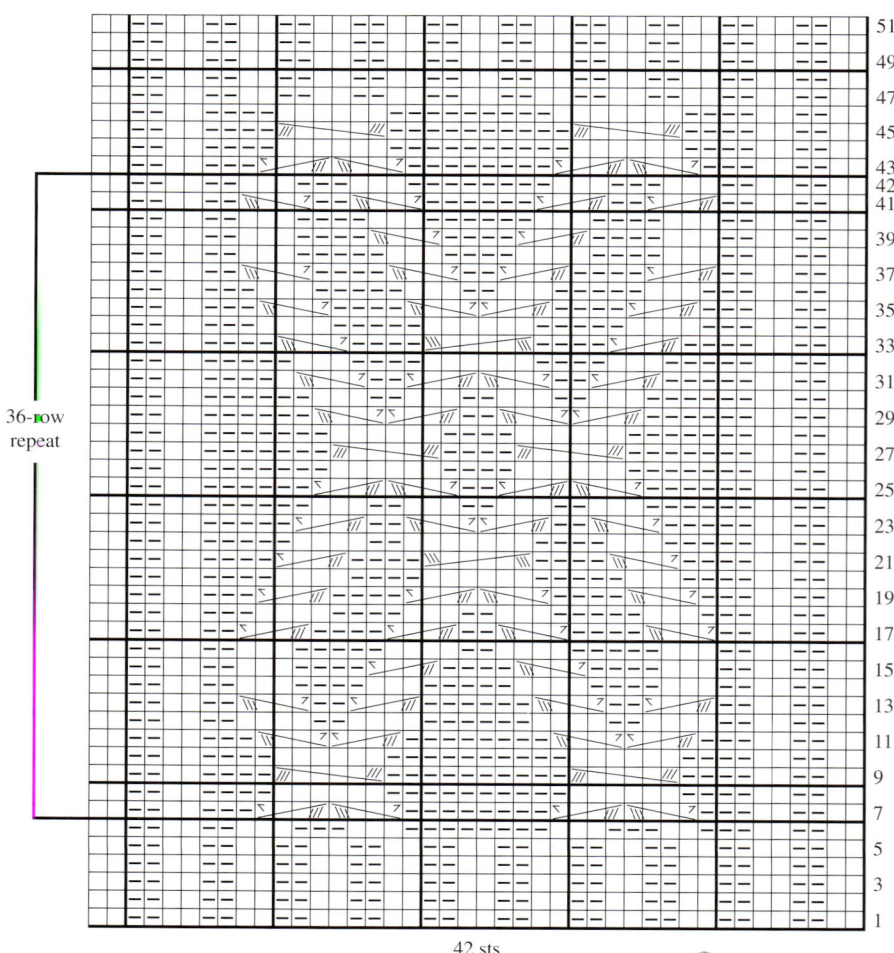

Stitch Key

- ☐ K on RS, p on WS
- ☐ P on RS, k on WS
- 4-St RPC
- 4-St LPC
- 6-St RC
- 6-St LC

36-row repeat

42 sts

TOOLKIT

YARN (5)

- 3½oz/100g, 225yd/202m of any variegated bulky mohair

NEEDLES

- One pair size 9 (5.5mm) needles OR SIZE TO OBTAIN GAUGE

Eye [4] Media

MEASUREMENTS

Approx 7½ x 56"/19 x 142cm

GAUGE

12 sts and 14 rows to 4"/10cm over drop st pat using size 9 (5.5mm) needles.
TAKE TIME TO CHECK GAUGE.

STITCH GLOSSARY

DROP STITCH PATTERN

Row 1 (RS) *K1, wrapping yarn 3 times around needle; rep from * to end.
Row 2 Knit, dropping extra wrapped sts.
Rows 3 and 4 Knit.
Rep rows 1-4 for drop st pat.

SCARF

Cast on 22 sts. K 3 rows. Work in drop st pat until piece measures 55½"/141cm from beg, or until there are a few yards left (enough for 3 more rows). K 3 rows. Bind off.